Copyright (

All rig

No part of this book may be r   _____, or stored in a retrieval
system, or transmitted in any form or by any means, electronic,
mechanical, photocopying, recording, or otherwise, without
express written permission of the publisher.

ISBN: 9798654458384

MEDICAL DISCLAIMER

The content of this book is provided for support and advice. It is not intended to and does not replace specific, professional advice.

You must not use the advice given instead of seeking a medical opinion, professional support or medication. If you have questions about any medical matter, or think you are experiencing a medical condition you should consult your doctor or other professional healthcare provider without delay.

Please also note that each case of anxiety is different, so this general advice may not be tailored for your exact needs.

CONTENTS

ABOUT THE AUTHOR

Lucy Smith is a Mental Health Advocate, Author & Podcaster supporting others with understanding and managing their anxiety after her own struggles.

Lucy invested years into researching how best to manage anxiety to free herself from her own, then put the research and experience to good use becoming a mentor for others. Lucy is also certified in Cognitive Behavioural Therapy.

You can read more about Lucy at her website where you can listen to the Stand Up To Anxiety Podcast and access free resources for support with your anxiety.

www.lucyjsmith.com

INTRODUCTION

I began to struggle with how I was feeling in my teens. Throughout school I had always felt shy and that I lacked confidence but I thought that was normal and something every girl went through. I thought it didn't matter, that I would grow out of it and had no idea how it would affect my life. I continued facing my life in the way I always had and for as long as I can remember was the "quiet one" of the group. I had just accepted this as who I was.

When I left school it began to get worse. I felt alone, lost, worried, stressed, and down and I didn't know why. I had no idea what had caused it and I didn't know how to change it. Looking back in my journals from 2012 to 2015, when I was 17-20 years old I was experiencing these emotions almost daily:

Upset and crying all the time.

Argumentative with family.

Not wanting to get out of bed.

Nervous around people.

Not wanting to leave the house.

Unenthusiastic about things I used to enjoy.

Feeling lonely and like I had no friends.
Can't talk about how I feel without crying.
Mood changes quickly.
Easily frustrated.

The day came where I was in a supermarket with my sister, Katy, and she wandered off and left me alone in an aisle. I hadn't told her how I had been feeling so she had no idea what would follow. The panic began. I was crying and sweating uncontrollably, my heart racing. I had no idea what was happening to me and how to stop it.

I got back into my car and was unable to drive. The feelings were so strong I felt unable to move. I didn't know what to do or who to turn to. That was when I made the phone call to the doctor. When they answered the phone, I just cried. I couldn't find the words to explain how I felt or the help that I needed. The receptionist said she would book me an appointment to talk to a doctor.

My appointment with the doctor was a bit of a blur. He asked me questions about my life and if there were any problems at work or home. The answer to both questions was no, there was no obvious problem that had caused me to feel this way.

From there, I had weekly appointments with a counsellor, who told me I was struggling with severe anxiety and depression, and lack of confidence. She also uncovered two huge fears I had of driving and being alone in public. Making that phone call was the best decision I ever made. While it was scary having to admit to a doctor and then a counsellor how I was feeling even though I didn't understand it, I am so glad I did it.

I began to work with the counsellor on overcoming my fear using a simple technique to face my fears every week. To face my fear of driving I picked my Nanny & Poppa's old house to drive to. It was somewhere that meant a lot to me and motivated me to go, I felt I could talk to Poppa while I was there, as he had died a few years earlier.

Picking this particular place made it even more special to me facing and overcoming my fear. I set out weekly facing this fear and it didn't come easy, on the second week a car nearly crashed into me. I stayed committed and stuck to doing exactly the same drive every week at the same time.

Over time the anxiety I felt before, during and after started to go down. It started as a 10/10 and within a few months it went down. My fear of driving had decreased and eventually disappeared.

I used the same technique for my fear of being alone in public places. After the panic attack in the supermarket with Katy I knew this was one that I had to overcome if I was to live a normal life. I chose a store that I enjoyed shopping in and committed the time to facing my fear weekly. I had the same results as the driving fear, within weeks the feeling of fear decreased before going down to zero fear. I can now walk confidently into any shop and spend time there without panic attacks or anxiety. Even if a panic attack does start I now feel I know what to do to get it under control and feel calmer.

The best thing that came out of seeing the counsellor was her recommendation I read the book Finding Peace In A Frantic World by Danny Penman and Mark Williams. At the time I hadn't even heard of mindfulness and the book was huge, which overwhelmed me, so I didn't read it. It did, however, help me to realise the world of self-help existed, making me interested enough to find out more.

I began to do my own research into personal development to find books that felt better for me and other habits that I could use to help improve the way I was feeling. I began to feel that I wasn't alone. I was glad to discover there was a reason I was feeling this way, which helped me to feel more normal and believe that there was a way I could get through it.

On my journey of personal development, I have created a morning and evening routine full of personal development that I stick to daily. It has become a habit to me and as important as brushing my teeth. I have come across many habits on this journey and have tried most of them. Some I enjoy, some I don't and that's okay. It's about finding the ones that work well and sticking with them.

I am now completely different to the person I was

back then. To my friends and others I am known as the "happy and positive one" - the complete opposite to the story of my childhood and especially secondary school years. I couldn't have achieved this without the world of self-help and for that, I will always be grateful.

Advice for you

It's not about getting rid of these feelings completely. I don't believe that mental health problems ever go away, they just need managing and that is what I feel I do so well now. Every now and then something will trigger anxiety, knock your confidence or give you a feeling of fear and that is okay. The important thing is knowing how to manage it. By putting together a 'toolkit' of tools and techniques, you can be prepared for when these feelings are triggered.

A morning and evening routine is a great way to do this by starting and ending your day in the best way possible. How you spend the first 30 minutes of your day can have a big impact on what follows, so you will set yourself up for a good day. The same goes for the evening, settling down with self-care and personal development before going to sleep, which can help you sleep well and wake up in a good mood. Personal development has the ability to transform your life. It starts with a decision and commitment to want to change.

How to use this book

This book is a guide to build your own toolkit of tools and techniques to use. I will walk you through all the habits I use daily. There are many exercises and questions in the book, so I suggest you get a journal to complete them all and get the best results. Try all the tools I suggest and see how you find them. Please note in this book the words tools, tips, techniques, strategies and habits are all used to mean something you can do or use to help with your anxiety.

Make a list of techniques that work for you and use them when you need to. The aim is to create an anxiety toolkit to use in moments of mild anxiety, severe anxiety, and panic attacks. Come back to this book when you need a refresher or to relearn any techniques.

In section 1, we'll cover understanding anxiety so you can begin to understand what is happening and why you feel the way you do. Then we'll move on to other things you may experience related to your anxiety, its potential effects and ways to manage them. Section 3 is all about learning new strategies and tools to manage your anxiety that you can try for yourself and judge the benefits. This will help you to form your own anxiety toolkit that you'll continue to use after finishing this book.

Make sure you get access to the free bonuses avail-

able with the book at:
www.lucyjsmith.com/book-bonuses
You will find workbooks to use to answer all the exercises in this book, journal prompts, affirmations for anxiety and a progress tracker.

Before we get started, fill out this questionnaire to assess how you are currently feeling. Answer all questions with either yes or no, then give yourself 1 point for every yes answer. Try not to think about it too much and write down the first answer that comes to mind.

Complete this questionnaire again at the end of Section 1, 2 and 3 to see your progress throughout the book. You can continue to use the questionnaire after you've finished reading to track your progress and how you're feeling.

Do you trust you can cope?
Do you use your breath to calm your mind?
Do you feel grateful everyday?
Do you feel present most of the time?
Do you protect yourself from negative people or things?
Do you know what to do when anxiety is triggered?
Do you make time for self-care most days?
Do you take care of your mental health?
Do you feel equal to others?
Do you love yourself?

SECTION 1: UNDERSTANDING ANXIETY

In this section you will learn how to start understanding your anxiety. You'll begin to understand the triggers, symptoms and patterns of your anxiety.

Let's start with some definitions so you can understand and put a name to what you are feeling.

Generalised Anxiety Disorder (GAD) - "A condition characterised by 6 months or more of chronic, exaggerated worry and tension that is unfounded or much more severe than the normal anxiety most people experience." [1]

High Functioning Anxiety - "People with high-functioning anxiety are often able to accomplish tasks and appear to function well in social situations, but internally they are feeling all the same symptoms of anxiety disorder" [2]

Social Anxiety - "Social anxiety disorder, also called social phobia, is a long-term and overwhelming fear of social situations." [3]

Panic Attacks - "Panic disorder is an anxiety disorder where you regularly have sudden attacks of panic or fear." [4]

It is important for you to know that you are not the only one struggling with anxiety, though it often feels that way. Approximately 1 in 6 people in England experience a mental health problem like anxiety each week.

UNDERSTAND
YOUR ANXIETY

Before you can learn how to understand and manage your anxiety you first need to accept it. Simply saying to yourself 'I have anxiety' is a good start. Whenever you experience anxiety and its symptoms remind yourself that you have anxiety and this is how it feels for you right now.

To understand your anxiety you need to know what it is, what triggers it and how it makes you feel. This will be an ongoing process and you will discover more about yourself and your anxiety over time. Anxiety is different for everyone and I don't believe there is a one size fits all toolkit for managing anxiety effectively.

You may learn that as you begin to understand and manage your anxiety something else comes up that triggers anxiety for you, when this happens add it to your journal so your list of triggers stays up to date. You will also learn tools that work for different situations and when it is best to use them.

According to the U.K.s National Health Service "anxiety is a feeling of unease, such as worry or fear, that can be mild or severe." [5]

To me, anxiety is feeling so worried that your body and mind begins to feel out of your control. That is how it made me feel. When my anxiety was triggered it felt so hard to get control over how I felt and stop the symptoms I experienced.

Spend some time reflecting on what you think your anxiety is. How would you define it? How does it make you feel? How often do you experience it? From these answers come up with your idea of what anxiety is to you. There is no right or wrong answer here, but it will be useful for you to come up with your own definition.

Exercise: what is anxiety to you?

Define what anxiety means to you.

When you understand what goes on in the brain and body when anxiety is triggered you'll realise why it makes you feel so bad. When we get feelings of anxiety the fight, flight or freeze response is activated and hormones are released that prompt us to either stay and fight or run, which is useful in a life threatening situation, when we need to make that decision to stay safe. However, it is not useful when the response is triggered by something like social situations, public speaking or even just thinking about something that worries you. The other reaction you may experience is to freeze. You may feel unable to move, not know what to do or even have an out of body experience.

While the fight, flight or freeze response is activated, the body is working to focus its energy on keeping you safe and alive. This explains why your heart rate and blood pressure quicken to get all the nutrients and oxygen to parts of your body that may need it. You may also feel on edge because you are more alert to danger and will be looking around for things that may be a threat.

Knowing when and how your anxiety started can help in understanding and managing your anxiety. Look back on your life and think about anything that happened that may have caused you to start feeling anxious. Think about the smaller events too, not just the bigger ones. Examples may be being bullied in school, an embarrassing performance in a play and family breakups.

Think about all experiences in your life that could have led to the anxiety you experience now, write everything down that you can think of whether it seems relevant or not. Start at the beginning and work your way through to where you are now.

Exercise: look back to where it began

Roughly when your anxiety started:

Make a list of all the events that you experienced and when:

RECOGNISE
YOUR ANXIETY

The symptoms of anxiety vary from person to person. You may also realise that you get different symptoms from different triggers, or even different severities of symptoms. This is why tracking your anxiety triggers and symptoms is a vital part of understanding your anxiety. The more you understand your anxiety the easier it will be to manage.

Health anxiety, a specific form of anxiety, can be triggered by feeling these symptoms. It is constantly worrying about your health, and wondering if there is something wrong with you. I have experienced this myself and it is important not to get overwhelmed when you feel any symptoms of anxiety. If you are experiencing severe physical symptoms for the first time it is recommended that you seek medical advice to get checked over.

When you feel any physical symptoms, remind

yourself that it is a normal reaction to anxiety and that it can be managed. The good news is that as you begin to manage your anxiety and find the tools that work for you, the severity of your symptoms may decrease over time. Even if your symptoms do persist, you can use them as a warning that anxiety is coming and to start using your techniques to get it under control.

The most common symptoms I have come across in myself and the women I work with are:

Physical symptoms: sweating, shaking, headaches, stomach aches, heart racing, dizziness, light-headed, feeling hot, finding it hard to breathe and feeling jumpy.

Cognitive symptoms: negative thoughts, dread, feeling worried or nervous, self-doubt, lack of confidence and feeling of the mind racing.

Behavioural symptoms: disturbed sleep, avoidance of activities, procrastination, difficulty concentrating, feeling restless or irritable, repetitive thoughts and disorientation.

Exercise: anxiety symptoms

What symptoms do you experience?

Symptoms may change over time or change depending on the trigger, so keep space in your journal to write down new symptoms to give you a clear and up to date idea of how your anxiety makes you feel. Then the next time you feel those symptoms you can look back at that page to remember that you are feeling them because your anxiety has been triggered.

Begin to recognise what triggers your anxiety and the patterns that emerge. Is it a certain place, person, event or situation? Hopefully, you'll know from previous exercises how your anxiety makes you feel so when you begin to experience those symptoms think about what happened directly before it started.

Potential triggers could be a crowded public place, public transport, having to speak in a meeting, phone calls, meeting someone new, an interview, driving, going to a new place, dreading an upcoming activity and thinking about something from the past.

Exercise: track your anxiety

Over the next few weeks track what triggers your anxiety. Record the symptoms and their severity. You can also write down any tools you tried to manage your anxiety and if they worked or not.

Date:
Time:
Trigger:

Physical symptoms:

Cognitive symptoms:

Behavioural symptoms:

Tools to manage and their effect:

When you have completed the previous exercise you can begin to look through them all and figure out what regularly triggers your anxiety. It may be that it is the same situation time and time again or it could be that many different situations trigger your anxiety. Make sure you leave extra pages in your journal to continue this exercise as you may discover more triggers over time.

Exercise: your regular triggers

Make a list of all the triggers that came up 3 or more times in the previous exercise.

Over time, current triggers may disappear, you may get new triggers or they may stay the same. Get into the habit of noticing any new triggers and adding them to the list so it is always up to date.

With your list of triggers you can see if there are any that you may be able to avoid, for example, if socialising with your work colleagues triggers your anxiety then you don't need to go. Missing this isn't something that will have a huge negative effect on your life as long as you still have other social interaction with those you feel comfortable with.

Naturally there will be some triggers that you simply can't avoid, one of my triggers was the job I had at the time but another was job interviews so I felt pretty stuck. For the situations you can't avoid that trigger your anxiety, use your toolkit of techniques to help you through, preparing for the event and using techniques to manage your anxiety.

MANAGE YOUR FEELINGS

I t is good to learn how to notice and name your feelings, this is the first step to being able to manage them effectively. Knowing how to manage your feelings is something that will help on your journey to managing your anxiety.

The Feelings Wheel is a way we can learn more words to describe how we are feeling rather than the usual 'happy,' 'sad' or 'worried' words we tend to use most often. Get into the habit of looking at The Feelings Wheel every time you feel something and find a word from the outside of the wheel to explain the way you feel. To view The Feelings Wheel go to

www.lucyjsmith.com/book-bonuses. [6]

Now that you have more words to describe how you are feeling you can begin to manage your feelings. Begin by noticing the way you feel, think about the symptoms you are experiencing, then find a name for this feeling, using The Feelings Wheel if you prefer.

Exercise: notice and name your feeling

How does it feel?

What is the name of the feeling?

When you start knowing how to notice and name your feelings you can begin to look into how to best manage these feelings. This can vary between people so try out a few different ideas and see what works best for you.

Begin to record the feelings you experience most often and anything you do to try and manage them. Use the techniques and strategies described later in this book to help with managing your feelings. Once you start using them you can learn which tools help you and which are less effective, remember it is different for everyone so give them all a go.

Examples:
When I feel nervous, breathing exercises help me to feel calmer.
When I feel worried, distracting myself with my favourite comedy helps.
When I feel worthless, writing down all my achievements and success makes me feel better.
When I feel annoyed, listening to calming music helps to control my anger.

Exercise: managing your feelings

Feeling:
Techniques that manage it:

Try to get into the habit of noticing how you feel throughout the day, when getting started you could set an alarm to remind yourself to notice how you are feeling. If you notice you are feeling a negative feeling that you want to change then try something to change the way you are feeling. As you get used to this exercise noticing and naming your feelings will become easier and you may even find yourself doing it naturally throughout the day.

The first step to taking back control and changing the way you feel is expressing your feelings. When we verbalise how we feel we can begin to accept it. It's equally important to express positive and negative feelings, so try to express when you feel excited, proud or grateful for example. This is a great thing to record in your journal, so you can look back over time and see all the positive feelings you've felt, this can help to cheer you up on a bad day.

You can express your feelings by talking to someone, a family member or friend who cares for you and that you trust. Speak to them about how you are feeling and why you feel that way if you know. Explain to them that this exercise is purely for you to express how you are feeling so they should just try to listen and not ask further questions.

If you are already seeing or plan to see a counsellor/ therapist then this is an exercise you can do with them. You can even make notes between appointments of all the feelings you've felt so you can show them. This will help you both to recognise any potential patterns or triggers in your feelings.

If you feel you can't speak to someone then journaling is another way you can express how you feel. Write down all the feelings you have recognised. If you can, also write down why they started. You can do this in as much detail as you like, either writing a simple list of words or full sentences about how you feel. There are more details on journaling in Chapter 14.

Summary of strategies to help manage your feelings:

Use The Feelings Wheel to discover more feelings. Notice and name your feelings. Record the techniques that help manage the feeling. Express your feelings by talking or writing them down.

BARRIERS TO MANAGING ANXIETY

Before we get into the practical ways to manage your anxiety, it's important to think about the potential barriers to managing it. Maybe you've already thought of some, for example 'how will I find the time?' 'Where do I start?' 'Will it even work?' We will cover all of these questions in this chapter before we move on so you will be ready to start your journey.

It is natural to have questions or doubts about this journey. The very nature of anxiety usually comes with the side effects of worrying, doubting and questioning everything. My hope is that, what you've learned so far about understanding your anxiety will have given you the belief that anxiety can be understood and managed.

One of the most common questions I hear is, *'How

will I find the time?' The honest answer is, we all have the same 24 hours in a day and we will spend our 'spare time' after sleep and work on whatever activities we prioritise or see as important. For some this may be relaxing in front of the TV or engaging in a hobby.

If time is one of your barriers, reflect on how you currently spend your time and see if there are any activities you can swap out or shorten to add these new habits in. It may be 30 minutes less TV in the evening, or not scrolling through social media as the first activity of the day.

As for *'I don't know where to start'* that's exactly where this book comes in and it's why you're reading it. I've been where you are now, I didn't know where to start and let me tell you it was hard. I was introduced to mindfulness by my counsellor and I found my own way from there reading books, articles and blog posts, listening to podcasts and You-Tube videos and added it all together to create what I now use as my anxiety toolkit.

The good news is, all I've learned in the last 5 years is in this book. So you don't have to go through the same amount of research and trial and error because I've already done it for you.

You could be thinking *'I've tried before and it didn't work'* and that may be the case. Maybe you've read another book or done your own research and what you found didn't help you much. This could have been because you weren't ready at that point to start this journey or maybe those specific exercises or activities just didn't suit you. The way I see it you've got nothing to lose by trying other ways and seeing if they work better for you.

Another thing you may be asking is *'Will this even work?'* I know it has worked for me and as I have said, everyone's anxiety and the tools that work for them are different. But if you commit to learning how to understand and manage your anxiety and try the exercises available I believe you will feel some kind of benefit. The aim of this book is for you to feel in control of your anxiety, to understand it and to create a toolkit to use when your anxiety is triggered.

Exercise: your barriers

Which barriers may affect your progress?

You may be worried about facing your anxiety and making the decision to speak to a doctor or getting referred to see a counsellor/ therapist. Please know that it is completely normal to feel worried about this, but also know that it is their job to support you so if you feel you need that support then you should get it.

If you are worried about making an appointment because you don't know what to say then try writing down your feelings, worries and triggers for a week or so. Then in the appointment if you can't find the words to explain what you want to say you can just show them. It will help you if you prepare for the appointment and have learned a bit about yourself and your anxiety so you understand it better.

I want to give you an idea of what to expect and what not to expect from seeing a counsellor, based on my own experience in the U.K. During my first appointment I was asked to fill out a questionnaire based on anxiety and depression, which asked questions relating to feeling "down" and "worried". From this the counsellor was able to rate my anxiety and depression as severe.

My counsellor asked a lot of questions to get to know me better and find out more about the causes and triggers of my anxiety. We used a lot of worksheets to track and rate my anxiety and evaluate my progress.

Counsellors should be non-judgemental, professional and knowledgeable at all times, though unfortunately this isn't always the case and you may find yourself with a counsellor that you can't trust and work with. If this happens, then ask to see a different counsellor as a good relationship based on trust is essential for counselling to work.

Counsellors cannot prescribe medication, only doctors can do this, so if you want to talk to someone about potential medication then make an appointment with the Doctor. I was prescribed a Selective Serotonin Reuptake Inhibitor (SSRI) antidepressant when I struggled with panic attacks so badly it affected my work. Everyone's experience with medication is different and there are possible side effects so always consult with your doctor before starting, changing or stopping any medication for your anxiety.

If you are planning on making an appointment with a professional about your anxiety you can prepare by writing down how long you have experienced these feelings, your triggers, symptoms and anything else you know about your anxiety. The more you can describe the better so they can have a clear picture of what's going on for you. It may help you to fill out the exercises from Section 1 in this book and take those to the appointment to explain your experience.

It's up to you to decide if you are ready to understand and manage your anxiety. I'm not saying it's going to be easy and it definitely won't happen overnight. It's about commitment, consistency and community. Being surrounded by others on the same journey as you will support and encourage you along the way. I recommend you joining my Facebook group so you have a supportive community and extra support from me along your journey.

Facebook Group: Anxiety Support Group

www.facebook.com/groups/lucyjsmith26

SECTION 2: EFFECTS OF ANXIETY

A nxiety can make people react in different ways, many of which you may not realise are linked to it. The good news is all of them can be managed when we learn to understand and manage our anxiety.

There can be many effects of anxiety, which can include overthinking and cancelling plans. Having anxiety could mean you are more likely to experience effects like these because of how it makes you think and feel. Before we get into some of the effects and how to manage them, spend some time thinking about any that you think you may have.

Exercise: notice the effects you may have experienced

What do you experience that you think are the effects of anxiety?

UNHELPFUL THINKING PATTERNS

As you become more aware of your anxiety, you may begin to notice any thinking patterns you have. These will describe the way you think. When you know what your unhelpful thinking patterns are, you can begin to challenge and change them to more positive ones. Here are a few of the most common thinking patterns, some of which you may recognise as your own.

Catastrophizing - this is one that is often associated with anxiety, when you get caught up in what might happen and before you know it you have imagined the worst case scenario and now believe that it is reality.

Should or must - believing that you should or must do something is often linked to comparing yourself to others and feeling like you are not enough. This can create unrealistic expectations of yourself that can add extra pressure and lead to higher levels of anxiety. Try to remove the words "I should" or "I must" when talking about things to do.

Generalising - this would be when you make a general statement from something specific, for example "I felt anxious at that party, so that means I will feel anxious at all parties now." This is not necessarily true but you believe it to be. Try to remember that all situations and events are different and can affect you in different ways. For all you know, you may love the next party you go to.

Jumping to conclusions - when you make a decision or judgement before getting all the facts and evidence first you are jumping to conclusions. This can lead to making rash or even wrong judgements about situations or people. Instead, try to take your time collecting all the facts before you make any decision.

Mind-reading - this is when you decide what other people think about you and allow yourself to think they are judging you in some way.

Focusing on the negative - often when struggling with anxiety, you may find yourself focusing on the negatives. This may be in a conversation with someone, for example, your boss, where the feedback was 95% positive, but you only hear the negative.

Think about your thinking patterns and the situations they show up in. For example a social situation may look like this:

Situation: a party

Feelings: worried and nervous

Thought: What if I fall over? What if I say something stupid? What if I spill something down my clothes?

Negative thinking pattern: catastrophizing

Exercise: your thinking patterns

Situation:

Feelings:

Thought:

Thinking pattern:

Challenge unhelpful thoughts

When you have recognised your thinking patterns you can begin to challenge your unhelpful thoughts. This is a five step process that you can follow step by step for each of the thoughts you want to challenge.

Step 1: Evidence for and against

Is there any evidence for or against your thought? For example, the thought "I'm a failure" could be proved false by evidence such as I passed my school exams, driving test etc.

Step 2: Type of pattern

Can you recognise this thought as part of one of

the unhelpful thinking patterns listed above? If so, write it down and name it as an unhelpful thinking pattern.

Step 3: Be a good friend
Think of the thought as something your friend is experiencing. What would you say to them? What support and encouragement would you give?

Step 4: A positive perspective
Is there a different way you could look at this unhelpful thought? A more positive opposite that could be proven as true?

Step 5: A proactive solution
Do something to help solve or stop this unhelpful thinking pattern.

If one of the thinking patterns you are seeing in yourself is focusing on the negative use the below exercise to help with seeing the positive.

Exercise: what went well?

When thinking about a particular event or situation that you are noticing as only negative, make a list of everything that went well. This will help you to realise how many positive things happened and change your outlook from negative to positive.

Overthinking is often associated with anxiety, when we get caught up in our thoughts so much that it is all we think about. When struggling with over-thinking it is a good idea to set a time limit on it. An activity that I call 'worry time' is where you set a period of time that you are allowed to worry. During this time allow yourself to overthink and worry about it without trying to come up with a solution. If you feel it helps you could write your worries down in a journal, which can often feel like a weight has been lifted. Any time you begin to overthink outside of your worry time remind yourself that it can wait until your worry time begins.

Summary of strategies to help negative thinking patterns:

Recognise your thinking patterns.

Use the 5 step process to challenge unhelpful thoughts.

Focus on what went well.

Schedule worry time if you are overthinking.

LACK OF CONFIDENCE

As someone that struggled with both I can see the link between anxiety and confidence. Feeling anxious can mean you feel less confident and lacking confidence can lead to anxiety, particularly social anxiety. I believe that building your confidence is a vital part of your journey to managing anxiety and that as you build your confidence you will be better able to manage your anxiety and the other way round too.

You may be lacking confidence in the way you look, act, speak or live. Try to recognise where you lack confidence.

Answer these questions to get a better idea:
Do you lack confidence in work? Why?
Do you lack confidence in your appearance? What area?
Do you lack confidence in social situations? When?
How do you feel about yourself?

How do you feel when you lack confidence?
When do you feel least confident?
How often do you feel a lack of confidence?

It's equally as important to focus on the positives and think about when you are confident.

Answer these questions to reflect on your confidence:
When do you feel most confident?
What area of your life are you most confident in?
What clothes do you feel confident in?
What was one occasion where you felt really confident?
What does confidence feel like to you?
Why do you want to feel more confident?

These are two of my favourite exercises for building confidence:
Visualisation - using your imagination to see yourself with more confidence, you can imagine this generally or in a particular situation where you want more confidence. (Details in Chapter 12).
Affirmations - creating positive statements in the present tense and saying them as if they are already true. (Details in Chapter 13).

A client came to me wanting to feel more confident so I recommended these two exercises. She decided to commit to them both every single day and within a short period of time felt her confidence was transformed. She was able to start the business she'd always wanted to do because she finally had the confidence to do it.

Exercise: visualise your confident self

Close your eyes and take a few deep breaths, allow yourself to relax. Once you feel relaxed and ready, imagine yourself in your mind, see yourself in as much detail as possible. See a particular event or situation where you would usually lack confidence, but this time see it all unfold with you having full confidence and enjoying the event. Visualise this in as much detail as you can and use all your senses. See what you are wearing, hear how you talk and what you say, even feel the way you would feel. When you have finished visualising take a few deep breaths and wiggle your fingers and toes to come out of the deep state of visualisation.

The way we talk to ourselves affects our confidence and unfortunately most of the time we talk to ourselves in a negative way. According to the National Science Foundation, around 80% of our thoughts every day are negative.[7] People with anxiety often say they experience repetitive negative thoughts throughout their day. Imagine the impact on our confidence and mental health if we added more positive thoughts.

It is definitely possible to talk more positively to yourself. The first step is to begin to notice your negative self-talk. Get into the habit of noticing it straight away and challenging it. Simply saying "stop" to interrupt it or asking yourself "is this useful right now?" and realising the answer is no may be a way to stop the negativity inside your head.

Sometimes you may need to do more to stop it, you could try writing down all the reasons it isn't true. When this is needed, get your journal and write down the negative statement you are saying to yourself. Then start to write down all the reasons that it isn't true, write down as many as you can think of. An example of this might be the thought "I am rubbish at everything." Some of the evidence against this would include qualifications you've got, tests you've passed and everything you've been good at in your life.

Another exercise you can do is ask yourself if you would speak to a child or your best friend in that way. If the answer is no then you shouldn't be speaking to yourself like that. Ask yourself what you would say to a child or your best friend and speak that way to yourself instead. Use this exercise to get into the habit of noticing when you are not being kind to yourself and changing the words you use.

You can use affirmations to reinforce positivity into your daily thoughts and self-talk. When a negative thought comes up in your mind replace it by saying the positive opposite of it on repeat. For example "no one loves me" becomes "I am loved."

If you are having a hard time believing your new

affirmations, consider altering them slightly so they feel more achievable to you. Continuing with the above example you could say "I am beginning to feel more loved" or "I am learning to accept love" See Chapter 13 for more information on affirmations and how you can create your own.

Unfortunately comparison is something a lot of people experience and it can really knock our confidence, particularly with all the media we are exposed to. We find ourselves looking at people's social media feeds where they always look amazing and never have any struggles. It's important to remember that this person chooses to only share the positives about their life and you're not seeing the whole picture.

This is why I openly share my struggles on social media, even now I have days where I struggle with my anxiety or a panic attack and I share this so you can see my life as honestly as possible. Go through your social media and follow people who share openly and honestly like this, especially others struggling with anxiety so you feel you aren't alone on this journey.

Exercise: clear out your social media

Look through your social media and unfollow anyone that makes you feel uncomfortable, triggers your anxiety or causes you to compare yourself to them. Then find new positive people to follow who inspire and support you.

You may also find you are triggered by seeing old school friends on social media and compare where they are in their life to where you are in yours. If you feel the need then unfollow them on social media, they won't find out you've done this particularly on Facebook where you can stay "friends" but just not see their posts.

Remember that comparing yourself to others is completely natural and everyone has done it at some time. When you catch yourself comparing, say "stop" and try to distract yourself with something else to get away from the comparison.

Spending time away from social media can help stop the constant comparison. On days where you look at social media and the majority of your thoughts include comparison of some kind, log off for the day and focus on yourself and your life, as staying on social media will only make it worse. You can then continue to use social media as normal the next day and see how you find it.

Exercise: have a social media detox

Plan time to put your phone away or remove the social media apps. Spend the day in the present moment without the distraction of your phone. If you enjoy this time, plan to do it more often.

In times where you feel you are comparing yourself to others take a minute to ask yourself if this is the full picture of their life. Remember the truth is they only share what they want people to see. It is impossible to compare the full movie of your life to the highlight reel of someone else's.

Exercise: what are you proud of?

Write a list of all the things you've done in your life that you are proud of. Continue to add to this list every time you think of something new. In time, you'll have pages full of all the things you have to be proud of and you can look through it when you need a reminder or positive boost.

Another way to look at comparison is as motivation, for example if you are comparing your life to someone else's, think about why that is. Do they have the job you want? If so, think about how you can start working towards getting that job yourself. Do they have control of their anxiety? Use that as motivation to commit to understanding and managing yours. Using comparison in a positive way like this is more beneficial than letting it upset you and negatively affect your life.

Summary of strategies to help with building confidence:

Visualisation.

Affirmations.

Notice and challenge your negative self-talk.

Unfollow triggers on social media.
Social media detox.
Focus on the positives in your life.

SOCIAL ANXIETY

Social anxiety is a fear of being watched, judged or rejected by other people, which can make social situations incredibly difficult. This could be triggered by something that happened to you, or by something that you worry about doing.

It is important to know that social anxiety is common and a lot of people struggle in social situations. When I'm out and I'm beginning to feel anxious in a social situation I like to look at all the other people around me and remind myself that they may be experiencing social anxiety too.

When struggling with social anxiety we can often get caught up in the worst case scenario, which most of the time isn't likely to happen. Changing the way you look at the situation can help you go into it with a more positive mindset and you will be better able to control any feelings of anxiety.

One good way to do this is to visualise it going as well as possible. Find a quiet place and sit down with your eyes either focused on a plain surface or closed if comfortable. Begin by taking some deep breaths and allowing yourself to feel relaxed. When you feel ready, allow yourself to see the situation unfold in your mind, watch yourself feeling calm and relaxed. Imagine this in as much detail as possible using all the senses so you really feel like you're there.

You may find yourself avoiding situations or events because they make you feel anxious, and as I said earlier occasionally this is okay, as long as it won't have a negative impact on your life. Connection is important for our mental health and we shouldn't cut out all social contact, so it's best to learn to feel more comfortable in social situations.

The more you do something the more comfortable you will feel. Doing things that scare you and managing them successfully will also help to build your confidence. The first step to facing these events that cause you social anxiety is to list them all.

Exercise: make a list

What events and situations do you avoid?
Schedule one thing to do this week:

Now that you have your list, schedule a time to do them. Start with the one that feels easiest for you as this will help to build your confidence to face the more intimidating ones. You can ask for support with this from someone who understands what you are going through and is happy to support you. For example if you avoid coffee shops ask a friend to go to one with you, then when you feel ready you can go to one on your own.

While you are there if you begin to feel anxious use some mindfulness or breathing exercises to help you to feel calmer. If you feel the need you can take a time out to give yourself a break.

If you find it helps try repeating your positive affirmations on repeat in your mind. This will help to reinforce positivity and the thought that you are okay.

Summary of strategies to help social anxiety:
Visualise the event going well. (Chapter 12)
Take a friend or someone supportive with you.
Prepare before the event. (Chapter 17)
Use positive affirmations. (Chapter 13)
Mindfulness exercises. (Chapter 12)
Take a time out if you need to.

PANIC ATTACKS

As someone with anxiety you may also find that you experience panic attacks. If you are experiencing one for the first time, or think you have experienced them, but haven't been checked by a doctor then do so, since other medical conditions have similar symptoms. Once you know you are suffering from panic attacks, you can begin to recognise, accept and cope with them.

Begin to notice what a panic attack feels like to you, so you can recognise your own panic attacks. Panic attacks can last any amount of time and can be of different severities with different symptoms.

My panic attacks were short and intense. An overwhelming feeling of fear, my heart racing, sweating, stomach churning and feeling sick. On occasions I felt dizzy, lightheaded and I collapsed. For hours, sometimes days after the panic attack I would continue to feel physical, cognitive and behavioural symptoms, particularly feeling drained, worried, on edge and jumpy.

Symptoms vary for each person but can include faster heart beat, chest pain, sweating, feeling sick, stomach churning, chills, hot flushes, trembling, feeling faint or shaky, dizziness, ringing in the ears, dry mouth, a choking feeling, tingly fingers and feeling disconnected from your body.

Exercise: write down your own panic attack experience

Date:
Time:
How long it lasted:
Trigger:
Symptoms:

When you are having a panic attack, accept it as that. Know that it is a panic attack, that it will pass in time and you will be fine again. If it helps write this somewhere so you can see it as a reminder. You could also ask someone to say this to you when you have a panic attack.

You'll begin to learn new strategies to help you cope in a panic attack, both from this book and other research you may do. Make a list of all the strategies that work for you so you can choose one without too much thought.

Some ideas of coping strategies for panic attacks:
Movement or exercise.
Go for a walk.

Close your eyes and take some deep breaths.

Use visualisation to go to your happy place.

Mindfulness exercises like focusing on your senses.

Muscle relaxation exercise.

Essential oils that make you feel calm.

Exercise: useful coping strategies for you

Make a list of all the coping strategies that have helped you in a panic attack.

Your 3 step method for panic attacks:

Step 1: Recognise it is a panic attack, know the symptoms to expect.

Step 2: Accept that it is a panic attack, know that it will pass and you will be okay.

Step 3: Use a coping strategy to calm the panic attack, know what works for you.

FEAR

One of the first things my counsellor uncovered was what I was afraid of. Everyone is afraid of something, sometimes many things, so fear is perfectly normal. It is when fear stops us from doing things and living our lives that it becomes a problem. My fears were driving and being alone in public places, particularly shops, both of which I had to overcome to live a normal life.

Exercise: recognise your fears

What are your fears?

The technique I used to overcome my fears was a simple one, that I call rating my anxiety. This is a great technique to use for fears like being in public places, social occasions and driving, where actually doing it will help you overcome it. I planned a time every week when I would go out and face my fear. Before I left, I rated how anxious I felt from 1-10. In the beginning it was very high, I felt very severe symptoms and like I was on the verge of a panic attack. I pushed through the anxiety and went to do it anyway.

When I got home I recorded the level of anxiety I felt during the event and anything that happened during the event. Finally, I rated the anxiety I felt after.

Over time my anxiety dropped during and after the event, because my catastrophizing thoughts were proved wrong. In turn my level of anxiety before the event began to decrease, because I had built up evidence that I was usually safe doing this activity.

Occasionally when doing this exercise something will happen that confirms the fear. For example, when I was using this technique for my fear of driving on one occasion a car nearly crashed into me. When this happens we have two choices - give up and stay afraid, or carry on trying to overcome it. I chose to overcome it and continued going out for that same drive every week until it became easier for me and I was no longer afraid.

Exercise: rating your anxiety to overcome a fear

Pick a date and time to do this exercise and add it into your calendar so you are committed to doing it every week.

Date:
Time:

Event:
Anxiety level before:
Anxiety level during:
Anxiety level after:
What happened during the event:

Sometimes, we are afraid of things that can't physically harm us, for example being afraid of someone's judgement. Although these fears feel completely logical and very real, it is important to recognise the difference between things that can actually harm us and those that can't. Either way facing those fears will make you realise that you can still do something that you are afraid of. Spend some time reflecting on your list of fears and figure out which ones can actually cause you any harm.

It is worth knowing that feelings of nerves and excitement can bring on the same physical symptoms, so you may be able to trick your mind into thinking you are excited about doing it. Put on your favourite music and dance around to get energised. You can even say to yourself "I am excited," which is a powerful affirmation to use.

Exercise: create a happy playlist

Put together a playlist of music that you can listen to when you need a boost of excitement and energy before doing something you are afraid of.

As someone who struggles with anxiety and fear,

you may find yourself dreading going to events you have planned, whether it is coffee with a friend or an upcoming family wedding. Often anxiety can take control and make it impossible to look forward to social occasions that you would have usually enjoyed.

To begin to work on not dreading these plans you need to take action to show yourself that it isn't as scary as it may feel. You need to prove to yourself that you will be okay and the only way to do this is to go. I know that may seem crazy but it works.

Make a list of all the events you dread going to and give them a difficulty score from 0 (lowest) to 10 (highest). Then put them in order and work your way through them, starting with the lowest scoring activity. Stay on that activity until it becomes easier, then move on to the next activity.

Exercise: face the dread

Write your list in order from lowest difficulty to highest. Tick off each activity as you face it.

By understanding your comfort, stretch and panic zones you can begin to push yourself to face your fears. The comfort zone includes the activities you find easiest and that you do without any feelings of fear.

The stretch zone includes the activities that give you some fear but are manageable, doing these activities regularly will mean you get more used to them and they may even move to your comfort zone.

The panic zone includes the activities that cause you uncontrollable fear or panic attacks, these are activities you will want to avoid as much as possible. However, the more you practise the activities in the stretch zone the more confidence and belief you'll have to face some activities in the panic zone.

You may find yourself in a situation where an activity you must do is in your panic zone. If this is the case, use the above techniques to face those activities regularly until they become more comfortable to you. You can also add any anxiety management tools and techniques you pick up from this book to help manage the anxiety you may feel during the activity.

Exercise: your zones

Comfort zone activities:

Stretch zone activities:

Panic zone activities:

Summary of strategies that help to overcome fear:
List all your fears.
Rating your anxiety technique.
Get excited instead of feeling afraid.
Face the events that you dread.

Know your comfort, stretch and panic zones.

SECTION 3: ANXIETY TOOLKIT

In this section you'll learn the daily habits I have tried myself during my journey to understanding and managing my anxiety. Your aim is to try out the ones you like the sound of and make notes about how or when they were useful. The more you record about the habits and how they help the easier it will be to create your own anxiety toolkit.

When getting started with adding new habits into your day I always recommend starting small with 1 or 2. Once you get used to doing these and you're feeling the benefit then it is time to experiment with adding more or trying different habits. It can be overwhelming to add too many habits too soon, which can have a negative effect on how you feel, on maintaining them and potentially, the results you'll get from this book. My biggest tip is to ease yourself in gradually and do what feels comfortable to you.

To start with, think about any daily habits that you currently have, whether good or bad. Maybe you've already started to add some in that you've learned from this book or other resources. Maybe you have some negative habits like scrolling through social media in bed in the morning or watching TV programs that trigger your anxiety.

Exercise: daily habits

Make a list of all your positive and negative daily habits.

SELF-CARE

Making self-care a daily habit is essential to your well-being even though often people feel that it is selfish to put themselves first. The famous saying, you can't pour from an empty cup, says it best, you have to look after yourself before you can help anyone else. This is true in home, work, social and all other areas of life. By making time for self-care you can become a better partner, parent, employee, friend and person for all those around you.

Self-care is any activity in which you look after yourself. This ranges from the daily care of yourself, making sure you eat and sleep well, to setting boundaries and saying no to someone when needed. Any activities you enjoy are also included, for example pampering yourself, reading, gardening or playing an instrument.

Exercise: write your self-care list

Make a list of all the activities that you like doing

that are considered self-care.

After making your self-care list, it's time to plan it into your day. Just thinking about it and writing a list won't be enough for you to commit to this new way of thinking straight away. It's best to block out time for self-care in your calendar or diary like you would for meetings or appointments. To start with I suggest keeping this small so you find it easy to commit to, 10 minutes here and there throughout the week.

If you're struggling to start or stay consistent, then try setting an alarm to remind you when it is time for self-care. Over time, you'll have a daily self-care routine that feels good. I consider all the habits included in this book to be a form of self-care, as they all help you to look after yourself both physically and mentally which will help to keep your anxiety feeling more manageable.

Many of these self-care habits can be used in moments of anxiety to distract yourself, this is one that works for some and not others so try it to see if it works for you. You can use any of these self-care habits, including watching your favourite film, comedy series or listening to a positive music playlist.

Another way that may work is to distract yourself with cleaning and decluttering the house. This can help to calm your anxiety and take you away from the worries in your mind, with the added benefit of a tidy house. I love the saying a clean house, a clean mind and believe it to be true.

Self-care is about looking after yourself physically, as well as, emotionally and mentally. Movement can change the way you are feeling. I have known people that move in some way when they feel a panic attack starting, to change the way they feel.

A 2018 study on the effects of aerobic exercise on anxiety symptoms concluded that regular aerobic exercise reduces anxiety levels. [8]

Yoga postures, known as asanas, can be used as a way to reduce the physical discomfort you feel when anxious. Yoga is a very calming exercise as it focuses on breathing while going through the yoga poses. It is also a way for the body and mind to feel connected, so as you go through the different poses you may begin to feel more in tune with yourself.

Walking can be beneficial to your mental health as walking regularly triggers the body's relaxation response which helps to reduce stress. It is a great exercise to do when your anxiety is triggered as it can boost your mood and energy. You can also use your time walking to practice mindfulness, which will be explained in more detail in Chapter 12.

Create breaks during your day for movement, especially when at work or sitting for a long time, setting an alarm to remind you to get up and move every hour.

Think about creating a workout schedule for you to do, whether at home or in the gym. I recommend starting smaller so it seems more achievable, and is easier to commit to. Search for workouts that you enjoy and save them somewhere you can access them easily when you need to.

If you can, partner up with someone. Committing to exercise can be easier with the support and accountability of doing it with someone else. Even if the person isn't near you and able to physically meet, you can let them know your goals and plans and ask them to hold you accountable.

Exercise: interesting workouts

Make a list of all the ways to move and workout that you are interested in trying.

As I've said before the best way to follow through with something is to schedule it into your calendar. Look at your schedule and find a time you are free for a workout. Now I know you're thinking 'there isn't time' but remember what I said earlier about us prioritising what we see as important.

If you don't have a clear block of 30 minutes, think about time in the day or week where you can swap an activity for exercise instead. Maybe you watch TV for 30 minutes in the morning or you spend time scrolling through social media. Replace this time with your workout and you get the double benefit

of removing an old, possibly negative habit and re-
placing it with a new positive habit.

Exercise: making time to workout

What can you swap for your workout?

Exercise has the added benefit of making us feel
really good during and after the workout. I recommend recording the workout you did and how it
made you feel in your journal. This will help to mo-
tivate you to do it again as often the build up to exercise is the worst part.

Exercise: workout reflection

Workout:
Length of time:
How it made me feel:

Summary of strategies for self-care:
Create a self-care list of activities you enjoy.
Commit to a self-care schedule.
Find workouts that you enjoy.
Schedule workouts into your week.

GRATITUDE

G ratitude is one of my favourite tips, because it is easy to do, doesn't take much time, and is really effective. There are a few different ways to practise gratitude that I will talk you through in this chapter.

In the beginning, feeling grateful can be difficult, especially on days when your anxiety feels very intense and it's hard to focus on anything else. Keep going even when it feels tough and if you can't think of anything else just feel grateful for the simple things, a roof over your head, clean water to drink, warm water to wash in. There are many things to be grateful for if we just look to find them.

Many studies have shown the positive benefits that gratitude can have, including a positive impact on mental and physical well-being, sleep quality and better management of daily stress. [9]

One of the best things you can do is start your day with gratitude the second you wake up. You can do this by reflecting on 3 things you are grateful for. If it is gratitude for a particular person or something they have done then reach out and thank them, this will give them a good start to their day as well.

If you enjoy writing, then you could write down the 3 things you are grateful for each day in your journal. This is particularly powerful when you are having a bad day and feeling that everything is against you as you can look back through your journal and realise everything you have to be grateful for.

Gratitude journal prompts to use when writing:
What was the best thing that happened today?
What did you enjoy doing today?
What was one kind thing someone did for you today?
What hobbies do you love doing?
What did you do well today?
What are you proud of?
What did you do to make someone happy today?
What did you see that was good today?
What are you most grateful for in your life?
What are 3 things you are thankful for today?

Exercise: writing gratitude

Write 3 things you are grateful for right now.
1.
2.
3.

If you like to get creative, one great idea is to create a gratitude jar. Grab an old jar, a pack of post-it notes or paper and add to the jar every time you think of something you are grateful for. This also gives you a great activity for New Years Eve as you look through and reflect on a whole year of gratitude.

Lastly, a really powerful exercise is to actually thank people when you are grateful for something they have done. Often we say thank you without even thinking about it. Change this to mindfully thanking someone, telling them how they have helped you and the effect they had. Sending someone a personalised message, note, or card will make them feel really good and also contribute to your own mental well-being.

Summary of strategies for gratitude:

Reflect on what you are grateful for.

Start a gratitude journal.

Create a gratitude jar.

Thank people more and send thank you notes.

MEDITATION

The practice of meditation can be very beneficial when wanting to manage your anxiety. Before we start, I want to make sure your expectations are realistic. Often, when we think of meditation we see someone sitting on a cushion, legs crossed, eyes closed and making a noise (known as a Mantra). While some people do meditate like this, it is not the only way. There are many different ways to meditate and it's important that you find a way you are comfortable with and that works for you.

The next thing you need to know is that the goal of meditation is not to clear your mind of all thoughts. The simplest way to think of it is allowing your thoughts to come and go without judgement, if you like you can think of your thoughts as clouds that move across the sky. Remember this when you start meditating, it can be easy to get frustrated with yourself and feel like you are doing it wrong, but I promise you aren't.

Another thing to note is that although meditation

is powerful and effective in moments of anxiety, it is even better if you meditate regularly, even in times you don't feel anxious. If you are not used to meditating and use it in a panic attack you may feel your symptoms worsen when you try breathing exercises. In the past, I have felt light-headed when doing deep breathing exercises. If this happens to you, then stop the exercise. Try it again when feeling calm and relaxed to get used to the feeling of deep breathing.

There are many different types of meditation and if you haven't tried before I would suggest you start with a guided meditation of some kind. Search YouTube or the free app 'Insight Timer' for guided meditations for anxiety. Pick one you like and try it everyday for a week.

I personally like Heart Activation Breathing, which is used to sync your heart and mind together with the electrical pulses beating in the same rhythm. This form of meditation is done with your hand on your heart and begins with your normal breathing pattern. You will find an audio of this exercise in the book bonuses at: www.lucyjsmith.com/book-bonuses

Once you get used to a guided meditation for anxiety, you can begin to research different methods of meditation and give them a try. I have stuck with guided meditation and the mindfulness exercises listed below but there are plenty more for you to try.

Mindfulness is a form of meditation and simply means being present in the moment and being aware of your thoughts, feelings, surroundings and senses. This can be done in many ways, and once you're used to it you'll find yourself in mindfulness exercises naturally throughout your day.

Mindfulness helps you to move out of the fight, flight or freeze response and into the resting part of the nervous system which slows the heart and helps you to feel relaxed. It can be helpful to try a mindfulness exercise when you begin to feel anxious about something as it can take you away from the thoughts and worries in your mind by focusing on something else.

Examples of mindfulness exercises:

Breathing exercises - focusing on your breath, either counting each breath or saying "in" and "out".

Mindful eating - using your senses to fully experience every mouthful you eat without any distractions.

Senses - observe the area around you looking for things you can see, hear, smell, taste and touch.

Body scan - focusing on each area of the body in turn and noticing how it feels. You can also focus on relaxing each area of the body.

Mindful walking - go for a walk and feel the way your feet feel on the floor. You can also add the senses activity to your mindful walk.

Exercise: go for a mindful walk

Find a natural area in which to walk, leaving your phone and other technology behind, so you are not distracted. Observe the area around you, for example listening to the birds, looking at the trees and smelling the plants. Allow yourself to focus on the sensations from your surroundings.

Exercise: grounding activity 5, 4, 3, 2, 1

In moments where your anxiety is triggered look around you and notice:
5 things you can see
4 things you can feel
3 things you can hear
2 things you can smell
1 thing you can taste

Another technique closely related to meditation is one we've already used - visualisation. The same areas of the brain are stimulated whether we're visualising or performing an activity, so visualising can be as beneficial. Then, when you come to actually doing the activity, it will feel less frightening because you've already gone through it successfully in your mind.

For example, if you feel anxious in social situations like going out for a meal with friends, you would imagine yourself in the restaurant, feeling comfortable, ordering your food confidently, chatting, making conversation easily and feeling good the whole evening.

Visualising can be difficult at first, you may find when you close your eyes you struggle to imagine what you want to, or maybe you can't see it in detail. Don't worry if that is the case, that's how I started too. As I've said before, it will get easier with practise, and will become more effective.

Exercise: visualise your happy place

Sit or lie comfortably and close your eyes. Allow your body to relax, focusing on each area in turn. Once you feel relaxed, start to imagine your happy place in as much detail as you can, as if you are there now. Focus on what you would see, hear, smell, touch and taste. Stay visualising this happy place for as long as you need until you feel calm and relaxed.

Exercise: shower visualisation

In the shower when the water is running off your body imagine it taking all your feelings of anxiety with it. Imagine them washing off your body and going down the drain with the water.

Summary of strategies for meditation:
Guided meditation.
Mindfulness exercises.
Body scan.
Grounding exercises.
Visualise yourself in situations that trigger your anxiety.
Visualise the shower washing away your anxiety.

AFFIRMATIONS

Unfortunately, a lot of negative internal voices come with anxiety. Although this is quite normal for those with anxiety it isn't something you have to suffer. Positive affirmations are the most effective tool I've found to help with negative self-talk.

Put simply they are statements about yourself written in the present tense as if they are already true. You can create statements about how you want to feel and things you want to achieve.

They should always only include positive words, for example "I am calm" rather than "I don't feel anxious" or "I want to feel free of anxiety." Ideally you don't want the word anxiety in your affirmation as you will be repeating it a lot.

Examples:
I am free.
I am in control.
I am safe.

I am loved.
I am worthy.

A lot of people in the Female Anxiety Support Facebook group use positive affirmations. One says that she has some she says to herself every morning, some for the end of the day and others that she uses when she feels anxious. She finds that her affirmations alongside positive self-talk help her to manage her anxiety.

One of the best ways to create positive affirmations is to think about all the negative things you regularly say to yourself then find the opposite of that statement to use as your positive affirmation.

Exercise: write down your negative self-talk

Over the next week write down all the negative things you say to yourself.

Now it is time to turn your negative self-talk into positive affirmations, by using the opposite words in your affirmations. For example "I'm worthless" becomes "I am worthy" and "no one loves me" becomes "I am loved."

If you can't think of the exact opposite, then come up with a word that you like and that explains what you wish to be true. The most important thing to remember is that they use present tense and positive wording, it is also useful for you to like the word and for it to mean something for you.

If you are struggling to believe your affirmation, re-member what I said earlier in the book and alter your affirmation so it feels more achievable for you.

Exercise: create your positive affirmations

Write the opposite of your negative statement as a positive affirmation.

You can use positive affirmations to help you to ac-cept the way you are feeling and work towards cop-ing with it. Here are some examples of what you can say to yourself when you feel anxious:

I have felt this way before and I got through it.

I know how to cope, I trust myself to get through this.

I accept this feeling.

I know this feeling will pass.

I can reach out for help if I need to.

Now that you have created your positive affirm-ations we need to get you believing them. The power of affirmations is that the more you think and say them the more you believe them to be true.

There are a few different ways to use your affirm-ations so try each of them and use the one that feels most comfortable for you. You may find that as you get used to your affirmations you switch tech-niques, and that is fine.

Think - say them to yourself in your head on repeat throughout the day, especially when negative self-talk starts.

Write - write them down daily in a journal, particularly in the morning and at night but also at other times when you feel you need to.

Speak - say them out loud so you can hear yourself saying them. At first this may feel odd and you may not sound convinced but over time this will get easier and you will sound more positive. There is no need to move to this stage until you are ready and it feels comfortable.

Listen - it's powerful to listen to them in your own voice so try recording yourself saying them. You can take this one step further and add some relaxing music to the recording, so you can use this technique as a form of meditation.

Say them in the mirror - now this one may scare you, it scared me. It is so powerful when you feel comfortable looking yourself in the eye as you speak your affirmation. I remember the first time I did this, I was in the bath and I caught my reflection in the mirror and decided to say my affirmation, I looked myself in the eye and I really believed my affirmation, I ended up crying because it was so powerful and I was so happy and proud of how far I'd come. Let this be a goal for you and know that whenever you're ready you'll experience this magical moment too.

Over time your negative self-talk may change and

you'll say new things to yourself. When this happens, make some time to create new positive affirmations based on the new self-talk.

Summary of strategies to use affirmations:
Create affirmations from your negative self-talk.
Think, write, say or listen to them.
Create new affirmations when needed.

JOURNALING

You've probably heard before that journaling is a good way to get your feelings out and I believe there's truth in that statement. Journaling can be useful if you struggle with talking to someone about how you feel or finding the right words. Your journal can be private, and you can just write whatever comes to mind.

When journaling, don't judge anything you think or write down, just allow it all to come out. You'll usually feel better once it's all out on the paper. There is no right or wrong way to journal so find a way that you enjoy and that works for you. I'm going to give you a few different ways to try.

Thoughts - simply write down all your thoughts onto paper, you can write each word that comes to mind or you can write in full sentences.

Brain dump - this one can be useful in the evening or middle of the night if you are having trouble sleeping and have a lot on your mind. Writing it all down on paper will help to quieten the mind and help you have a restful night's sleep.

Positive journaling - flip your journaling experience to the positive, which is especially powerful if you have just journaled about all your negative thoughts and feelings. You can challenge the negative thoughts and write a positive reflection instead, such as a lesson you have learned from the negative situation you just experienced. Or if you have written down a load of negative self-talk, write down all the evidence that shows it is not true.

Gratitude - write down all the things you have to be grateful for, this is recommended first thing in the morning for maximum benefit to start your day feeling really positive.

Affirmations - write your affirmations in your journal.

Bullet journaling - this may be useful to you when you start using some of these daily habits. A bullet journal can be used to track your consistency with new habits by ticking them off once you've done them each day. You can also use a bullet journal to track your feelings daily, by colour coding different feelings and marking each day. This is a great way to get creative and use colour, if that is something you enjoy.

On days where you are struggling to come up with words to explain how you feel, try drawing a picture, or colouring something to show how you feel. For example use colours that explain your feelings or draw a picture of what your mind feels like.

Another form of journaling is letter writing. You can write letters in many different ways and for different reasons. A powerful technique is to write a letter to yourself, full of compliments. You could also try writing a forgiveness letter to a younger version of yourself or someone else that you need to forgive. It is up to you whether you then send this letter or do something like burn it to mark the end of it. Forgiveness is a very powerful exercise that will help you to move on from the past.

My anxiety began shortly after my Poppa passed away, so I would write to him in my journal, just chatting about everything going on to try and take my mind off my anxiety. I would also write in there about how I was feeling before I told anyone else, as I felt it was safer in my journal talking to him when I wasn't ready to share.

> **Exercise: positive journaling**
>
> What happened?
>
> How do you feel?
>
> How can you turn this to a positive experience or lesson?

If you struggle with writing in a blank journal or

don't know how to start then try using some journal prompts. Look back in Chapter 6 for journal
prompts for confidence and Chapter 11 for gratitude journal prompts.

Journal prompts for anxiety:

How are you feeling today?
What are you worried about right now?
What is on your mind?
What bad things happened today?
What is your anxiety telling you?

Journal prompts for self-love:

What good things do your friends say about you?
What is your favourite personality trait?
What are three things you are good at?
What is one thing you like about yourself?
What are you proud of?

Many members of the Female Anxiety Support Facebook group find journaling useful. Jessica said she
finds journaling easiest before bed. She lists everything she accomplished, anything that is worrying
her, a list for the next day and finally everything she
is grateful for. Dawn said she keeps a journal to write
in when she feels upset and another member said
they find it useful to journal daily about how they
feel and everything they are grateful for.

Summary of strategies to use for journaling:

Don't judge what you write in your journal.
Write your thoughts or do a brain dump.
Positive journaling.

Write gratitude and affirmations.
Start a bullet journal to track your progress.
Write a letter to yourself or to someone else.
Use journal prompts to help if you want to.

MORNING ROUTINE

One of the first things I did was create a morning routine as my anxiety was usually already high when I woke up. I decided to use that time for positive habits to help calm my anxiety before my day began.

You may be thinking that a morning routine isn't for you because you don't like to get up early or you're just not a morning person. Even if this is the case, I recommend you try adding positive habits to your morning and see what happens. If you don't like it or it doesn't help you can stop, but at least you'll know you've tried it.

To get started think about how you will make the time for your morning routine. Start by committing to a small amount of time, maybe 10 or 15 minutes as starting with too much time can be overwhelming. If you feel you don't have15 minutes spare, then consider setting your alarm for

15 minutes earlier to make the time, or reflect on how you currently spend your morning and see if there are any habits you can swap out to make time, for me this was watching the news and scrolling through social media, both of which triggered my anxiety.

Next, think about the habits you want to begin, you can pick any that have been mentioned in this book or any others you've found. It's all about finding habits that you enjoy and that help you to manage your anxiety. This is trial and error, so try different habits until you find what works best. Again, I recommend starting small so it doesn't feel overwhelming, usually 1 or 2 habits is the best amount to start with.

Once you have a routine that you are happy with, stick with it everyday. Doing your morning routine at the same time everyday will help it to become a habit. If you do this daily for at least 21 days it will become easier, more natural, and you'll begin to wake up feeling ready to step into your morning routine.

Even when you're used to your morning routine and getting consistent with it, there may be days where you wake up and struggle to get it done. Know that this is normal and be kind to yourself, it is okay to miss a day if you really feel you need to. If you can try to get at least 1 habit done that day so you feel you achieved something and feel the benefit from doing it.

Over time, you may learn about new habits or want to change your morning routine. When you feel this urge, try new habits, swap them in and see how that feels. You can even add more time to your morning routine when you feel ready.

Think about ways to get motivated for and stay consistent with your morning routine. Here are a few ideas:

Set an alarm - put your alarm clock or phone away from your bed so you have to get out of bed to turn it off. Set another alarm after the one that wakes you up, so if you haven't already started it you will be out of bed and ready to begin.

Bullet journal - get a bullet journal so you can track your daily habits and tick them once you have done them each day. This is also a good way to notice if you miss the same habit regularly so you can swap it for one you will enjoy more.

Connect with why - think about why you want a morning routine and how you want to feel when you wake up. You can even write about this in your journal. Also, write in your journal how you feel during and after your morning routine, so on days you don't fancy it, you can read that as a reminder of how you'll feel after it's done.

Tell the people in your house - this is a great way to let everyone in your house know what you are doing to manage your anxiety and ask for their support. You can ask them to hold you accountable and use this as a time to check in with them about how you're feeling and ask for any support you need.

Accountability partner - find someone else that wants to commit to a morning routine. You use the Female Anxiety Support Facebook group for this and post in the group what your morning routine is then come back and comment on your progress.

Get a Mentor - as an Anxiety Management Mentor, I support women with creating and getting consistent with their morning routine, evening routine, and self-care, so if this is something you're interested in then get in touch with me to discuss more.

Sample morning routines:
First thing in the morning - wake up to the alarm and get straight into the habits.
After school drop off - when back home start your morning habits.

Recommended morning routine habits:
Exercise - any type of workout that gets you feeling energised for the day, details in Chapter 10.
Meditation or visualisation - detailed in Chapter 12.
Journaling - any of the techniques listed in Chapter 14.

Exercise: your morning routine

Time:
Habits:
How it makes me feel:

During a 1:1 session Emma wanted to find a way to stop her "crash and burn" feeling some weekends after a busy week of work. I suggested starting the day with some personal development and self-care. Emma decided to commit 30 minutes of her morning to 4 new habits and we made a plan of this with timings. After we set the plan we talked about potential obstacles that would prevent Emma from committing to this and we also planned to get around these by setting alarms and using the group as accountability. Emma enjoyed her new morning routine and found that she felt a lot calmer and more in control of the day. She kept it up for a while, before slightly adjusting it to suit her better, changing to just the two morning habits of yoga and meditation which she continues to do now.

Summary of strategies to create a morning routine:

Pick an amount of time that you can spend on it.
Start with 1 or 2 habits that you enjoy doing.
Stay consistent by telling others about it.
Set alarms as a reminder.

EVENING ROUTINE

S leep is something that you may struggle with because of your anxiety, but it is also something that can help you to manage your anxiety. Getting a good night's sleep is important when learning to manage your anxiety, as the daily events and situations you face will feel harder the less sleep you have had.

The quality of your sleep can be improved by having an evening routine to help you wind down and relax before going to sleep. Studies have shown that the blue light from screens like the TV and your phone will negatively affect your sleep quality as well as the health of your eyes.[10] Because of this, I recommend having a period of time away from technology before going to sleep.

In the modern world, it is considered normal to watch the TV in bed while scrolling through social media or catching up with the news, however,

I want you to use this chapter as an opportunity to reflect on these activities and the effect they have on your anxiety, mood and sleep. I know for me, it had a very negative effect, causing me sleepless nights, nightmares and midnight panic attacks.

Choose a time that you will switch off all technology. I know this can be a big change and others in your house may not agree or want to do the same, but choose a time for yourself and they can make their own decision.

There are many relaxing activities that you can choose to fill this time with instead:

A warm bath - you can add some bath salts, essential oils, and candles if you like them. Use this time to de-stress and practice mindfulness, using all the senses to enjoy the moments of relaxation.

Stretches or bedtime yoga - light stretches are a great way to help the body and mind relax, especially if you are feeling tense. Make sure you search for "bedtime" stretches so they will be appropriate for relaxation and sleep.

Read - pick a book that you really enjoy, whether it is a self-help book or one in a genre that you enjoy. I highly recommend it being a positive or light book rather than crime, horror or intensely emotional, as the last thoughts of your day will stay with you overnight.

Gratitude - spend some time reflecting on all you

are grateful for that day using any technique in Chapter 11.

Meditation - try a guided meditation or deep breathing exercise for extra relaxation during your evening. A body scan is a great way to help the body to relax ready for sleep. Details in Chapter 12.

Visualisation - use visualisation to help relax the body and mind. You can visualise a relaxing place that makes you feel calm. For example a beach or lying in a hammock. Visualisation exercises are explained in Chapter 12.

Colouring - treat yourself to an adult colouring book to use in the evening. You can use this time to get creative and relax.

Music - create a relaxing music playlist that you can listen to during your evening routine or even as you fall asleep.

Sleep meditation - if you really struggle with dropping off to sleep try a sleep meditation to help you relax and fall asleep. You can search for sleep meditations specifically for anxiety and listen to these to fall asleep, or when you wake up in the night.

A 1:1 client, Emily, struggled with anxiety and panic attacks at night. We talked about creating an evening routine that would help her to fall asleep easier and some strategies she could do when she wakes up in the middle of the night. Emily chose to commit the last 30 minutes before bed to an evening routine including reading, gratitude, and a sleep meditation. As extra motivation, Emily chose to reward herself if she completed a week of this evening routine by getting her nails done. Emily found that her sleep quality improved and she knew what to do when she woke up in the night with a panic attack.

Exercise: your evening routine

Amount of time:
Habits:
How it makes you feel:

Summary of strategies to create your evening routine:

Set a time to stop using technology.
Commit an amount of time before bed.
Pick habits that make you feel relaxed.

YOUR ANXIETY TOOLKIT

On some occasions, an event or activity that triggers your anxiety can't be avoided. When this is the case, the next best thing you can do is prepare. For example, if you are going for a meal at a restaurant you haven't been to before you could look online at the menu to decide what you will eat, look at directions to the restaurant and parking nearby, ask a friend to go with you if possible, speak to others going to the meal and share your anxiety (if you feel comfortable doing so) and plan what you will wear before the day comes so you don't have to think about it.

Preparation is also key when thinking about how others can help you when you are experiencing severe anxiety or a panic attack. Speak to people close to you who are happy to help and explain to them how they can help you best. You could even have a list of things for them to do as you know during the time you won't be able to tell them how to help. Here are some ideas for your list, add anything else that would help you and remove the ones that you don't find as effective, everyone is different.

How to help me:
Reassure me
Give me a cuddle
Let me cry
Listen without judgement
Don't ask questions
Encourage me to breathe deeply
Take me out for a walk
Put on my happy music playlist
Put on my favourite comedy show

You can prepare yourself for occasions of high anxiety with a box of things you find useful to manage your anxiety. You can add to the box over time with different resources and tools to help you. For example, a self-care ideas list, DVDs, books, meditation CDs, photos of happy memories and a journal.

Alternatively, create a digital list with links to meditation audios, visualisation exercises, workouts, and other resources you find useful.

When you are experiencing a bad day and it feels like everything is triggering your anxiety and you can't control it, allow yourself to accept it for what it is - a bad day. Then you can begin to use the coping strategies you have learned in this book, as well as any preparation you have done like the box of anxiety management above.

Preparing to tell someone about your anxiety can seem scary and you may not even know where to start. It is important that you tell family, friends and even your boss what you are experiencing to help them understand and support you better. You may give some only a basic overview while others get the full story, that decision is up to you based on your relationship with and trust in the person.

Make a list of all the people you feel need to know, then decide how much you want to tell. You may find this easier if you have a 'diagnosis' so if you haven't already considered getting professional help then I suggest you do, not only will this help in your recovery, but it will also help others to understand if you can tell them what a doctor or counsellor has said.

Before you explain to someone else how you are feeling, it is good to have an understanding yourself, hopefully the exercises in this book have helped. If not, don't give up hope, there is still time. It takes a while to fully understand your own anxiety so be patient and trust it will happen for you. Simply saying "I have anxiety" or "I am experiencing panic attacks" will do until you feel able to explain it in more detail.

When talking to close family and friends, you could go into more detail about your anxiety triggers and the symptoms you experience. If you feel comfortable, you can share your exercises from this book with them. When they fully understand how you are feeling they will be better able to support you through it.

It is important to remember that not everyone will understand what you are going through. If this is the case then don't use that person as part of your support system, accept them as someone that doesn't understand or want to understand mental health and focus on the people that do want to support you.

My hope is that you have begun to understand your anxiety more, know how you can begin to manage it and that your answers to the exercises in this book have helped you explore your anxiety.

Exercise: check in

What have you learned about your anxiety?

Continuing all that you've learned from this book will be the most effective way to understand and manage your anxiety.

This means continue to:
Record your symptoms.
Track your triggers.
Try new management techniques and list what works.
Use your anxiety toolkit in moments of anxiety.
Track your progress.

As I've explained before, your anxiety may change

over time, some triggers will stop, new ones will start, and some will always remain, so keeping an up to date list of your anxiety triggers, symptoms and techniques will help you to manage it as effectively as possible. If you started a journal to go with this book and completed the exercises, then continue to use that and do the exercises regularly. You can also use the journal to track your progress of understanding and managing your anxiety.

Exercise: your anxiety toolkit

What habits and strategies are in your anxiety toolkit that you will use when needed?
Mild anxiety:
Severe anxiety:
Panic attacks:

WHERE NOW?

Now that you have finished reading this book you may have started to understand your own anxiety and know some ways to manage it. Going forward just continue to repeat what you have learned in this book.

You may be feeling overwhelmed by the amount of habits and ideas suggested in this book so just take your time. Start small and add more when you feel ready, as adding too much too soon may overwhelm you and have a negative effect. To keep it simple for you here is a checklist that will help you going forward.

Your checklist:

Track your triggers and symptoms.
Optional morning and/or evening routine.
Anxiety toolkit with techniques to use.
Reach out for support when you need it.

I hope you have found this book useful and that you now understand your anxiety more and feel you have the resources to manage it. After my own experience with anxiety, I wanted to make it as easy as possible for you to go through this tough time and feel there is a way out the other side.

Get the book bonuses at www.lucyjsmith.com/book-bonuses

Please keep in touch, you can connect with me here:
www.lucyjsmith.com
Facebook page: Lucy J Smith
Facebook group: Anxiety Support Group
Instagram: @lucyjsmith_26

NOTES

NOTES

REFERENCES

1.https://www.medicinenet.com/script/main/
art.asp?articlekey=23938
2.https://www.bridgestorecovery.com/high-func-
tioning-anxiety/
3.https://www.nhs.uk/conditions/social-anxiety/
4.https://www.nhs.uk/conditions/panic-disorder/
5.https://www.nhs.uk/conditions/generalised-
anxiety-disorder/
6.https://www.pinterest.co.uk/
pin/21884748168977565/
7.https://medium.com/the-mission/a-practical-
hack-to-combat-negative-thoughts-in-2-minutes-
or-less-cc3d1bddb3af
8.https://www.ncbi.nlm.nih.gov/pmc/articles/
PMC5827302/
9.https://positivepsychology.com/neuroscience-
of-gratitude/
10.https://www.ncbi.nlm.nih.gov/pmc/articles/
PMC6288536/

Printed in Great Britain
by Amazon